Life in Tudor Times

The Tudor Court

Jane Shuter

Heinemann

First published in Great Britain by Heinemann Library
an imprint of Heinemann Publishers (Oxford) Ltd
Halley Court, Jordan Hill, Oxford OX2 8EJ

MADRID ATHENS PARIS
FLORENCE PRAGUE WARSAW
PORTSMOUTH NH CHICAGO SAO PAULO
SINGAPORE TOKYO MELBOURNE AUKLAND
IBADAN GABORONE JOHANNESBURG

© Jane Shuter 1995

Designed by Ron Kamen, Green Door Design Ltd, Basingstoke, Hampshire
Printed in Spain by Mateu Cromo Artes Graficas SA

99 98 97 96 95
10 9 8 7 6 5 4 3 2 1

ISBN 0 431 06749 X [HB]

99 98 97 96 95
10 9 8 7 6 5 4 3 2 1

ISBN 0 431 06771 6 [PB]

British Library Cataloguing in Publication Data
Heinemann Our World Topic Books. - Life in Tudor Times. - Tudor Court
I. Shuter, Jane
942.05

Acknowledgements
The Publishers would like to thank the following for permission to reproduce photographs:
British School, Tate Gallery: p. 18C
Fitzwilliam Museum: p. 5B
Fotomas Index: p. 4A
Glasgow University Library, Dept of Special Collection: p. 27B
Guildhall Library: p. 17C
J Allan Cash: p. 21D, p. 7C
Marquess of Bath: p. 24A
Museum of London: p. 9C
National Portrait Gallery, Scotland: p. 12B
National Portrait Gallery: p. 6B, p. 8A, p. 22A, p. 28A
Simon Wingfield Digby, Sherbourne Castle: p. 14A
The Mansell Collection: p. 13D
The National Trust Photographic Library: p. 10A
The National Trust: p. 11C
Victoria & Albert Museum: p. 11B

Cover photograph © Fitzwilliam Museum, Cambridge/Bridgeman Art Library

Our thanks to Mike Mullett of the University of Lancaster for his comments in the preparation of
this book.

Every effort has been made to contact copyright holders of any material reproduced in this book.
Any omissions will be rectified in subsequent printings if notice is given to the Publisher.

Money
12 pence (d) in a shilling (s)
20 shillings (s) in a pound (£)

CONTENTS

1 What was the Court?

The **Court** was the name for the **monarch** and all the people who lived and worked with the monarch. The people of the Court were called **courtiers**. England and Wales were run from the Court. The **Privy Council**, which ran the day-to-day government of the country, met at Court. Its members were all courtiers.

People went to Court to get something from the monarch. Men wanted **places** (jobs) and favours. Women wanted places and to find rich, powerful men to marry. The Court worked like a pyramid of power. The monarch was at the top and all power came down from there. Next came the richest, most important **nobles**. Some of them were even related to the monarch. These people were given the important places at Court and could suggest people to fill the less important places.

Who went to Court?

Any **gentleman** could go to Court to try to get one of the less important places. He was not likely to get one unless he had a **patron** to ask for a place for him. People who came to Court without a place had to pay for their own food and lodgings. They could not afford to do this for long. They were the least important courtiers. The monarch fed and housed everyone who had a place at Court.

If the monarch liked them, courtiers could climb up the pyramid of power and become rich and powerful. But they had to be careful. The monarch made them rich and powerful but could also take all the money and power away. Courtiers had to please the monarch and not upset any of the powerful nobles, who might try to turn the monarch against them.

Source A

This picture shows a water entertainment given for Elizabeth I by the Earl of Hertford in 1591. It was an honour for a noble if the Queen (and the Court) visited them. But the entertainment often cost so much that they had to borrow money which they could not pay back.

17 July 1537

Madam, as Queen Anne ate the **quails** you sent she spoke of you and your daughters. My Lady Rutland and my Lady Sussex, who waited on her, both spoke well of you and your daughters. Queen Anne says you must send them both here and she will keep the one that suits her best. Until she has chosen they will stay with my Lady Sussex and my Lady Rutland. I think they have been much your friends here.

Part of a letter to Lady Lisle, wife of the Lord Deputy in Calais. It shows the importance of friendship among courtiers, which was strengthened by giving presents. Lady Rutland and Lady Sussex were patrons to Lady Lisle's daughters. Queen Anne was Henry VIII's wife.

This picture shows the palace of Nonsuch, one of Elizabeth I's favourite palaces. Her courtiers did not like staying there. The palace was so small that most of them had to live in tents in the palace grounds. The men in front of the palace are playing bowls.

2 Thomas Wolsey, 1475–1530

Thomas Wolsey's story shows how the son of an ordinary man could become powerful by using his position at **Court**. It also shows how much a **courtier** depended on the **monarch**'s favour.

Wolsey's rise to power

Wolsey was a clever boy. He went to Oxford University and he became a **priest**. He was **chaplain** to several **nobles** of Henry VII's Court. In 1507 he was made Henry's chaplain. But Henry died in 1509. The new King, Henry VIII, had his own chaplain. He gave Wolsey a less important job at Court. Wolsey worked hard to impress the new King.

In 1510 Wolsey was made one of the **Privy Council**. Henry VIII saw Wolsey was good at organizing and gave Wolsey more important jobs to do. In 1513, Wolsey helped Henry plan a war against France. England won. Henry made him chief adviser and gave him many important jobs in Court and in the **Church**, all of which paid a lot of money. Henry asked the **Pope**, Head of the Church (who lived in Rome), to make Wolsey a **cardinal**. Cardinals advise the Pope and choose the new Pope when the old one dies. Wolsey was the only English cardinal at this time.

Source A

Wolsey saw a clear path to **promotion**. He was so polite that he soon got a **place** on the King's Council. He was the quickest of all of the Council to do as the King wanted, no matter what. Soon the King valued him more than all his other Councillors.

A description of Wolsey's first steps to power, from a biography of Wolsey, written 27 years after Wolsey died.

Source B

CARDINAL WOLSEY

A painting of Thomas Wolsey in his cardinal's robes. The Pope made Wolsey a cardinal in 1515.

The gateway to Hampton Court, Wolsey's grand palace. Henry VIII added the clock after Wolsey gave him the palace. Hampton Court was one of Henry VIII's favourite palaces.

Wolsey in power

By 1515 Wolsey was the most powerful man in the country, except for the King. Most of the important courtiers came from rich and important noble families. They hated Wolsey because he came from an ordinary family, yet had more power in Court than they did.

Wolsey built himself a palace, Hampton Court, that was as grand as a royal palace. He made more enemies at Court by the ruthless way he trampled over everyone else to get Henry VIII what he wanted. As long as Wolsey succeeded, the King gave him more power and more rewards. Then Henry told Wolsey he wanted to **divorce** his wife, Catharine, and marry again. Wolsey asked the Pope for a divorce for Henry. The Pope refused.

Wolsey loses power

Wolsey had failed. Henry dismissed Wolsey as Chancellor (chief adviser). Wolsey was desperate to keep Henry's favour – he gave Henry Hampton Court as a present. But this was the moment all his enemies had hoped for. To turn the King against him, they accused Wolsey of over forty different crimes. Wolsey was found guilty, but Henry VIII let him keep some of his jobs and houses.

Wolsey's enemies feared that he might get back into Henry's favour. So, in 1530, they accused Wolsey of **treason** (plotting against the King). He was told to come to London to answer the charge. He was taken ill and died on the journey there.

3 William Cecil, 1520–98

William Cecil's father and grandfather had both been at **Court**, slowly working their way up to more important jobs. William followed the usual steps of a **gentleman**'s son on the way to a job at Court. He went to **grammar school**, on to Cambridge University, and then to learn law at the **Inns of Court** in London. He was clever, and enjoyed law work. He worked as a lawyer in one of the special royal law courts, the Court of Requests. In 1547 he became an **MP**.

Cecil was given several Court jobs under Edward VI, including a **place** on the the **Privy Council**. In 1553 Edward VI died. Mary, his eldest sister, should have become Queen but some Protestant dukes made Lady Jane Grey Queen instead, because Mary was a Catholic. Cecil disagreed with this. He resigned. Lady Jane Grey was Queen for nine days, then Mary took over the throne. She chose her own Councillors, but she used Cecil as an **ambassador** abroad.

Source A

Source B

This **judgement** I have of you, that you will not be **corrupted** by any gifts, and that you will be a faithful servant of the state.

Elizabeth I said this when she **appointed** Cecil as her chief adviser in 1558.

A painting of William Cecil, from the 1560s, possibly by Arnold van Brounckhorst. Although he had to wear clothes that showed he was important at Court, Cecil dressed as plainly as he could. He did not want to compete in fine dressing with the Queen, or with her favourites.

Some late sixteenth century posy plates or roundels. They were used in rich houses to serve sweet, sticky cakes at the end of a meal. One side was decorated, the other had verses or lines from the Bible on them. Cecil had some like this made especially for a visit by Elizabeth I.

Cecil and Elizabeth I

While Cecil did not do much work for Mary, he was in charge of running the **estates** of the Princess Elizabeth, Mary's sister. He wrote to her regularly about this. Elizabeth thought he was loyal and efficient. When Mary died in 1558 and Elizabeth became Queen, she made Cecil her chief adviser at once. He kept this job until his death in 1598.

Cecil's job was not easy. He did not always agree with Elizabeth, but advised her to do what he thought was best for the country. He did not always persuade her to do what he suggested (he could never talk her into getting married), but she trusted him and often took his advice. Cecil had a wife and family, but he saw little of them, for his work at Court took up most of his time. He was given land and power and his daughters married sons of **nobles**, but (unlike Wolsey) he was careful not to seem too important. He made sure that his new house, Theobalds, was no grander than other noble houses built at the same time.

Elizabeth was fond of Cecil. She gave him nicknames, like 'my Spirit', agreed that his son, Robert, would be chief adviser after him and, in his final illness, even visited him and fed him by hand. After he died she could never hear his name mentioned without crying.

Be humble, yet generous to your **superiors**. Be friendly and respectful to your equals. Be kind to those who are not as important as you.

Advice given by William Cecil to his son Robert on how to succeed at Court. Robert was Cecil's second son, and followed him as Elizabeth's chief adviser.

4 Bess of Hardwick, 1518–1608

Men came to **Court** looking for jobs that would give them land and power. Women came looking for husbands. People were more likely to die young then, so many people married several times. The story of Bess of Hardwick shows how women could use the Court to marry themselves, and their children, into **noble** families.

When she was fourteen, Bess married the son of a local **gentleman**. He died a year later and left her a large **estate**. She went to Court and married the Marquis of Dorset. They had three sons and three daughters. The Marquis died in 1557. Bess returned to Court and found her third husband, Sir William St Lowe. He loved her so much that he left her all his money and land when he died, leaving nothing to the rest of his family. This was unusual, and made them angry. Bess was now very rich. She went back to Court. The Earl of Shrewsbury fell in love with her. She refused to marry him until he agreed to two weddings between their children by earlier marriages. As soon as this was done she married him. Three months later Mary Queen of Scots fled to England. Queen Elizabeth I put the Earl of Shrewsbury in charge of her.

Building to keep alive?

Bess spent a lot of money building houses. It is said she did this because she was told by an **astrologer** that she would not die as long as she was building something. In 1608 her builders stopped work because of bad weather. She travelled in the cold and wet to tell them not to stop. She caught cold and died before they could start again.

Source A

We do not know who painted this sixteenth century portrait of Bess of Hardwick. It was obviously painted near the end of her life.

Sent to the Tower

Mary and Bess became friends. Bess married one of her daughters to Mary's brother-in-law, Charles Lennox, without asking Elizabeth I or the Earl of Shrewsbury. Elizabeth was angry. She had no children to rule after her and Charles was her cousin. He (or any children he had) might be the next **monarch**. Elizabeth expected to be asked about the marriages of important people like this. She put Bess in prison in the Tower of London. Bess talked her way out. In 1590 Shrewsbury died. Bess was now the richest woman in England. She never married again. She spent her time until her death, in 1608, planning marriages for her grandchildren, running her huge estates and building houses. The grandest of these was Hardwick Hall.

When the Earl of Shrewsbury was put in charge of Mary Queen of Scots in 1569 he was told to 'keep her busy'. Mary and Bess both embroidered well, so they spent a lot of time together, with their women, sewing. This elephant is just one of the pictures they made. Bess was accused of plotting, not just sewing, with Mary. She convinced Elizabeth that she was innocent.

Source C

Hardwick Hall, Bess of Hardwick's grandest house. Her initials 'ES' are in the decorations along the roof line. Many **courtiers** spent more money than they had on houses they did not need. They did this to entertain the Queen and the Court. Bess built Hardwick to show off her wealth.

5 Growing up

Tudor babies were expected to be as little trouble as possible. Parents had many more children than they do today, partly because they expected that several of their children would die young. People at the time did not know it was important to keep clean. They did not have as many medicines as we do now, and they did not have as wide an understanding about what causes disease. Babies and children were often sick. Once they were sick they were much more likely to die than children are today.

The fact that babies often died does not mean that parents did not care for them, or worry about them. Rich families could buy books that gave advice about problems like **teething** and **fevers**.

Source A

For easy growing of the teeth, cover the gums with a mixture of hare's brains, goose fat and honey. Give the child a horse's tooth, or a piece of **coral**, or other hard stuff to wear around their necks to chew on.

Advice on how to help a baby's first teeth come through easily. From _The Book of Children_, written in 1544 by Thomas Phaire. This book was still being printed and used over a hundred years later.

Source B

Cornelia Burch, two months old, painted in 1581. Babies were swaddled (wrapped tightly in cloth) for the first few months of their lives. This kept them still and quiet and was said to make sure their bones grew straight.

Tudor children were expected to grow up quickly. They were dressed in adult-style clothes as soon as they were no longer **swaddled**.

Preparing for Court

Nobles' children were prepared for life at **Court** from an early age. They had very little time to play with toys or in the gardens of their homes. Girls learned to dance, sing, play an instrument and sew. Many of them also learned to speak French. Boys also learned dancing and music. But they also had to be able to read and write, to speak several languages, to hunt and to fight.

Many nobles' children were sent to live with other noble families, to learn how to behave and so that other nobles could meet them. After this they went to Court. Once there, some married quickly and went to live on their country **estates**. They seldom came to Court again. Others stayed at Court, hoping the **monarch** would favour them.

A sixteenth century print of a tutor with his pupil. Nobles' children were often taught at home by a tutor. The boy is learning his alphabet from a horn book. The bundle of twigs is to beat him with if he does not learn fast enough.

Source C

To ride well, to **joust**, to be able to use all weapons, to run, leap, wrestle, dance well, to sing and play all instruments tunefully, to **hawk**, hunt and to play tennis are all necessary for a **courtier**. Also he should learn several languages, so as not to be outdone by the Queen.

A list of the things that a courtier should be able to do before he arrives at Court. This was written in 1570 by Roger Asham, who was Queen Elizabeth I's tutor when she was a girl.

Source D

13

6 On the move

The **Court** was always on the move. It moved around the royal palaces, which were all close to London. One reason for this was so the palaces could be cleaned. Tudor homes had no **sewers**, and no rubbish collection. Most of the palaces were by the River Thames, and a lot of the rubbish and **sewage** was thrown into the river. Even so, they got smelly and dirty very quickly. When the Court moved on, huge numbers of servants moved in to clear out the dirt and rubbish and leave the empty rooms to air.

What was a progress?

All the Tudor **monarchs** moved from palace to palace and visited various parts of the country if there was a special reason. Elizabeth I was the first monarch to make regular progresses (tours of the country) staying in royal palaces and **nobles'** houses. She travelled mostly in the south-east, and she sent paintings of herself all over the country. She often made plans and then changed them. The people of Leicester were promised a visit four times. They spent a lot of money preparing for the visit each time, and each time it was in vain. The nobles Elizabeth stayed with had to make even more complicated plans to entertain her than the towns she visited did. Some nobles built special houses, with rooms for the Queen and extra large rooms for the Court to meet in.

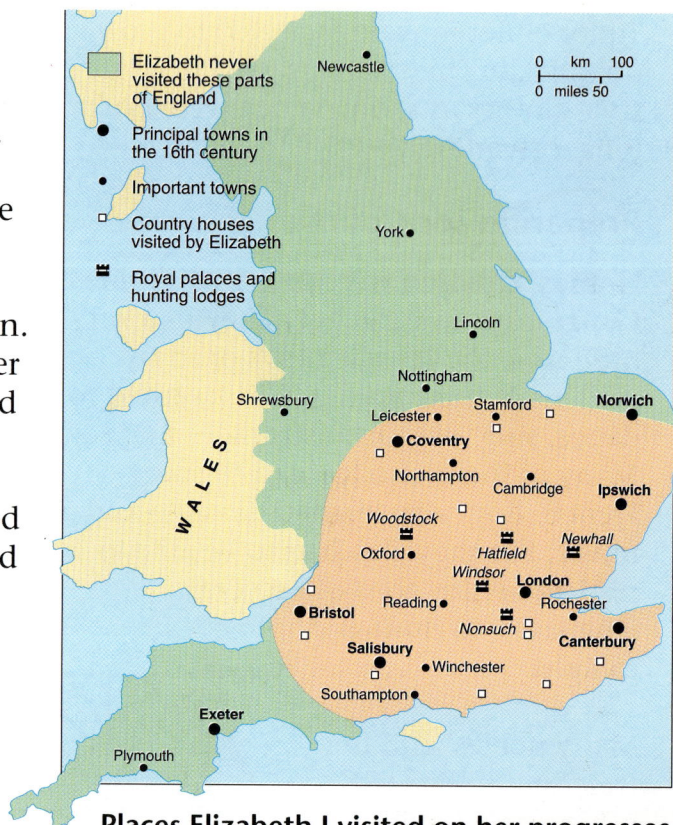

Map key:
- Elizabeth never visited these parts of England
- ● Principal towns in the 16th century
- · Important towns
- □ Country houses visited by Elizabeth
- ♛ Royal palaces and hunting lodges

Towns marked: Newcastle, York, Lincoln, Nottingham, Shrewsbury, Leicester, Stamford, **Norwich**, **Coventry**, Northampton, Cambridge, **Ipswich**, Woodstock, Newhall, Oxford, Hatfield, Windsor, **London**, Reading, Nonsuch, Rochester, **Bristol**, **Canterbury**, **Salisbury**, Winchester, Southampton, **Exeter**, Plymouth. WALES.

Places Elizabeth I visited on her progresses.

Source A

This painting, made in about 1600, shows Queen Elizabeth I being carried by her **courtiers**. When she went on a progress she would ride in a coach and be carried like this for processions through towns and cities.

Nobles tried to avoid a visit from the Court. A visit was an honour, but it was also very expensive. People who could not build a house for the visit still had to provide food, beds and entertainment for everyone and presents for the Queen. Nobles also tried to avoid going on progresses. The Queen was always made comfortable, but most of the rest of the Court were not. But the Queen loved progresses. She was seen by her people, had a chance to go hunting, and did not have to feed and house the Court.

67 sheep
34 pigs
4 stags and 16 bucks (for 176 pies)
1,200 chickens
363 capons
33 geese and 6 turkeys
2,844 pigeons
a great many pheasants and
a partridges
many cartloads of oysters and fish
2,500 eggs
430 lbs of butter

Some of the food Lord North ordered for a three-day Court visit.

7 A place at Court

Courtiers all wanted a **place** at **Court**. The number of places varied from **monarch** to monarch. Henry VII's Court had hundreds of people; Elizabeth I's had over 1,500.

There were many different sorts of Court places. The most important involved the most work, but had the biggest rewards. People who had these places also had a lot of power, and could often **appoint** other people to less important places. For instance, the Court was run by three men. The Master of the Horse organized all the transport. The Lord Steward organized the food, the cleaning and the sleeping arrangements. The Lord Chamberlain organized the daily life of the monarch and entertainments. They had to work very hard, and take the blame if things went wrong. But they were paid a lot. They were also given presents by the monarch and by people who wanted their help to find a place.

There were also places at Court helping to run the country. The monarch's Councillors had to give advice and carry out royal decisions. They also had to talk to Parliament for the monarch and meet **ambassadors** from foreign countries. Less important jobs included running the special royal law courts or just dealing with all the letters that arrived for the monarch and the Councillors.

Many Court places just involved keeping the monarch and the royal family happy. All queens needed ladies-in-waiting – women from **noble** families who kept the Queen company. They dressed her, sang with her, sewed with her, read with her, hunted with her and did whatever she wanted to do.

There were also courtiers who were rewarded with a place at Court because they could entertain the monarch or even talk them out of a bad mood.

Source A

8 October 1523

I hear the Duke of Albany is preparing to **invade** from Scotland. The young nobles at Court should come here to risk their lives for their king, and if not, be seen as little but dancers, dicers and cardplayers.

Part of a letter from the Earl of Surrey to Cardinal Wolsey. Noble courtiers were expected to fight when England was threatened, especially under the early Tudor monarchs.

Source B

November, 1594

Good Mr Hicks, the bearer of this letter, Isaac Burgis, has asked the Lord Treasurer for a place in the escheator's office (a law court that dealt with land disputes). I know he is a good **clerk**, and recommend him.

Part of a letter from Baron Ewes to Michael Hicks, a secretary to William Cecil, who was then Lord Burghley, the Lord Treasurer. To get a place at Court you had to have a patron who knew a courtier with power.

This painting shows a meeting of the Court of Wards. This was a law court that chose people to look after rich children whose parents had either died or could not look after them. Appointing guardians for wards was an important decision, because whoever got the 'wards' (the children) ran their **estates** and could make a lot of money from this. They also often decided who their wards would marry.

8 Marriage

Courtiers, especially those from **noble** families, were expected to marry. They had to marry someone from a similar family, richer and more noble if possible. Some marriages were arranged by the families while the bride and groom were still young. Couples were betrothed (made a promise to marry) long before the wedding. However, couples were not often forced to marry. The usual age for them to marry was when the girl was about nineteen and the boy was about twenty-three.

What changed?

Marriage hardly changed the life of male courtiers. They could leave the **Court**, but they were not expected to and they could not hope for many royal favours if they did. Women often left Court when they married, they seldom came back once they had children. Women were expected to have lots of babies. Most families of courtiers had five or six children. The wife had more babies than that, because many of the babies born at this time died before they were a year old. Not all the children in a family were likely to have the same parents.

Diseases were more common and more likely to kill people. Having babies was quite dangerous and many women died. So many people married more than once.

Most courtiers married for reasons other than love. But many of them worked happily together to run their families and **estates** and some were lucky enough to have long and happy marriages.

Source A

How old were courtiers when they married?

	Men	Women
1550–74	23	20
1575–99	23	19

This table shows the average age at which nobles got married for the first time. Girls could marry from twelve onwards, and boys from fourteen, but most did not.

I thank you for your good will, but I pray you be content, speak no more to me of your love. For that depends wholly on my parents. For if I am not ruled by them in my marriage they will no longer support me.

From a letter written in about 1558 by a young lady to Thomas Wythorne, a courtier who was musician to several Court families. It is a reply to a love letter he sent her. He was not as rich as her family. She married a richer man.

The painting shows twin sisters from the Cholmondeley family, who both had their first baby on the same day. It was painted in about 1600. Their clothes are similar, but not exactly the same. The babies are tightly swaddled.

9 Houses and homes

The homes of Tudor **courtiers** changed a lot in Tudor times. When Henry VII became King in 1485, the English **nobles** had been fighting and changing kings almost non-stop for many years. Most nobles lived either in castles or in houses that were so well defended that they were very like castles. Things that made a home safe (small windows, thick stone walls and deep ditches around the house) were more important than things that made it comfortable.

How houses changed

The Tudors brought peace to the country. This meant that nobles and **gentlemen** began to build houses that were comfortable and grand, with large gardens and parks. The nobles who built the grandest houses lived in the safest parts of the country. Some people, like those who lived near the Scottish **border**, did not change their homes much. They still needed to defend themselves against the Scots.

During Tudor times nobles and gentlemen also made their homes more comfortable by filling them with more furniture. They bought more clothes, bedding and **plate** (mugs bowls and plates made from gold, silver or pewter). Houses were often draughty and the walls (often wood-lined) could look very dull. So courtiers covered their walls with huge **tapestries**, which added colour and warmth.

Source A

The **cardinal** has a very fine palace, where one has to go through eight rooms to reach the room where he will see you. The walls of all these rooms are hung with tapestries, which are changed once a week. He always has a sideboard filled with gold and silver plate, worth some 25,000 ducats.

Written by the Venetian ambassador to his masters in Venice, after a visit to Hampton Court in 1519. A ducat was an Italian coin. It was worth the same as a workman's monthly wages.

Source B

The houses of the nobility are now made from brick and stone. They are so grand that the home of the least important noble is now as great as a royal palace once was.

Written by William Harrison, in 1577, in *A Description of England*. Harrison worked for Baron Cobham for a time. Lord Cobham and his family are in the picture on page 25.

Source C

In noblemen's houses it is not rare to see rich wall hangings, silver vessels, and so much plate as to fill several cupboards, often to the value of £2,000 at least. All their stuff together is almost impossible to put value on.

Written by William Harrison, in 1577, in *A Description of England*.

Nobles' homes

Most noble families had more than one house. These houses were the manor houses on their estates. These houses were often added to and changed as time passed and family needs changed. Most families had a favourite house that was their proper home. The biggest and grandest of all the homes of courtiers were built during the reign of Queen Elizabeth. They were often built by people who were rich, rather than noble, courtiers.

Parham Park, one of the homes of the Palmer family. Various members of the family had posts in the Courts of Henry VIII and Elizabeth I. Most nobles had more than one home.

10 Family life

Noble Tudor families were much larger than families are today. They were organized into **households**. The household of a Tudor **courtier** was, like the **Court**, a pyramid of power. At the top was the head of the family who owned everything and had all the power and money. Then came his children and, once they married, their families. Their importance depended first on their sex (boys were more important), then on their age (the eldest was most important). The eldest son would inherit the **estate** and the place as head of the family. But, until his father died, he still had to obey his father, even as an adult.

Households could also collect **widows** or unmarried women who were related to the head of the household – aunts, sisters and sisters-in-law could all become his responsibility. There were also children of other families who came to live in the household and anyone who had been given a **place** serving the head of the house. After them came the people who ran the estates and the household and below them came the servants. Some servants were more important than others, too. The maids who looked after the ladies in the house were more important than the girls who scrubbed the pans in the kitchens.

Household duties and rights

Everyone in the household had **duties** that were clearly set out. They also had **rights** which were just as clear. The head of the household had the most power, but he had the greatest responsibility, too. He had to care for everyone in the household and make sure that they were well fed and provided for.

A painting of Sir Thomas More and his family. It is a copy of a painting by Holbein, made in the 1530s. The copy was made by Rowland Lockley in 1593 for More's son, who had the four people on the right (members of the family by 1593) included.

Source B

I have asked Mr Waterhouse to ask you to let my son have his education in your household. I hope this will bind him to you and your family in friendship and that he can learn from your wisdom and benefit from your advice.

Part of a letter written by the Earl of Essex to William Cecil, then Lord Burghley, in 1576. Courtiers often took the sons of other courtiers or gentlemen into their households to teach them how to behave at Court and help them to find a place there.

11 Eating and entertaining

Courtiers feasted a lot, at **Court** and at home. Eating and drinking well showed how rich and important a person was. Foreign rulers and **ambassadors** were often invited to Court feasts. These feasts were very grand. Where a person sat at a feast showed how important they were in the Court. The closer a person sat to the **monarch** the more important they were. Visiting rulers always sat with the monarch. Ambassadors could tell if their country was in favour with the monarch, or if the monarch wanted a favour, by where they were given a seat. Courtiers ate huge amounts of meat of all kinds. Meat was seen as food for the rich. Vegetables were for the poorer people, who could afford nothing else. This diet was very unhealthy. Some courtiers had scurvy from not eating enough fresh fruit and vegetables. One sign of this was that their teeth fell out.

Entertainment

Courtiers spent a lot of time dancing, especially in Elizabeth I's time. They also listened to and played music – both Elizabeth I and her father, Henry VIII, were skilled at music. The Court always attracted entertainers. Henry VII's accounts show that he was entertained by a Spanish acrobat, a tightrope walker and by a man who 'ate coals'. Elizabeth I liked plays and in her reign the Lord Chamberlain was **patron** to a group of actors called 'My Lord Chamberlain's Men'. They acted for the Queen and the Court in various big halls. One of these actors was William Shakespeare.

Tudor courtiers also had more active pastimes. They rode off to spend the day hunting deer or **hawking**. Tournaments (competitions) were held on special occasions, where they practised skills like **jousting** and **archery**. How much time they spent on things depended on what the monarch enjoyed doing – Henry VIII enjoyed tournaments because, as a young man, he took part. Elizabeth I preferred hunting.

Source B

The **nobles** eat much meat daily. Not only beef, mutton, veal, kid, pork, rabbit and chickens, but also venison and such fish and game as is in season. There are often some forty people sit down to dine in a noble house.

Written by William Harrison, in 1577, in *A Description of England*. Harrison worked for Baron Cobham for a time. He only discusses the meat the nobles eat, as if it is the only important thing.

Lord Cobham and his family, painted in 1567. The lady on the left is Baron Cobham's sister, who was part of the Cobham household. Fruit was very popular, and the Cobhams had their own orchards, as did many courtiers.

12 Health

Tudor doctors used a mixture of medical ideas. They believed that the way the planets moved affected people's health. So it was important to work out a patient's **horoscope** as part of the treatment. They also believed that the body had to have a balance of four humours in it to be well, and that the elements (earth, air, fire and water) affected these humours. The zodiac signs (which horoscopes were divided into) were ruled by the elements. So the elements, planets and humours all affected each other. Humours were also affected by the four seasons – some cures worked best at certain times of the year. These cures often meant making people vomit, or bleeding them – taking out some blood. They also used herbs, spices and other powders to treat sickness.

Source A

It is spring. He is hot and sweaty. He has too much blood. I must bleed him.

Yellow Bile

HOT AND DRY

SUMMER

FIRE

Blood

SPRING

AIR   EARTH

WATER

Black Bile

AUTUMN

WINTER

COLD AND WET

Phlegm

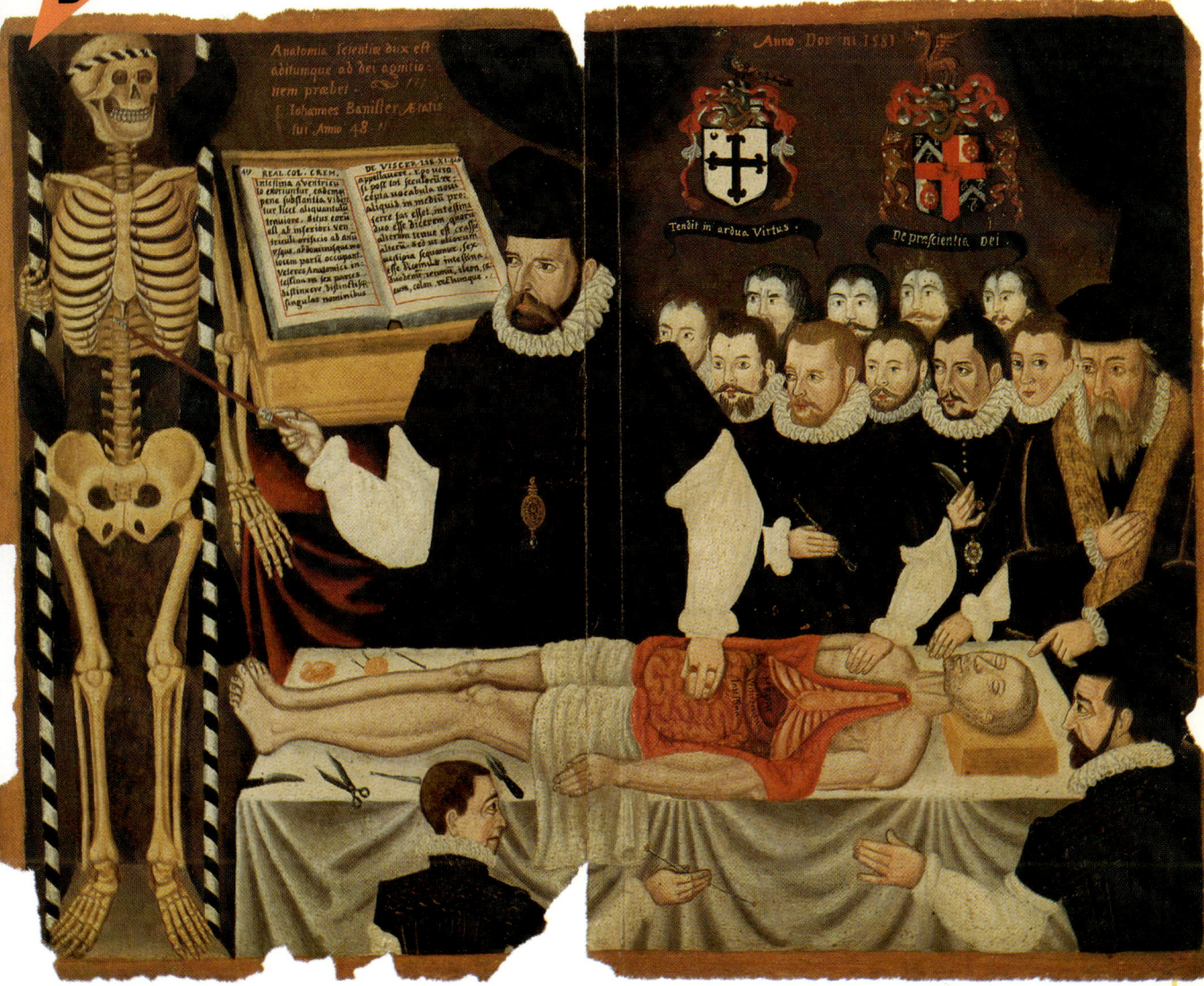

Her Grace's body has many cold, waterish humours. They require purging, but midsummer is the worst season of all for this treatment. She should wait until October to be bled and purged. Until then she must take care over what she eats.

A report to Queen Mary about the health of her sister, Princess Elizabeth (who became Elizabeth I), in June 1555. Mary sent her own doctor, Dr Owen, to look after Elizabeth.

This painting shows John Banister, a surgeon who wrote several medical text books, giving an anatomy lecture to other surgeons in 1581. People did not often have surgery. There were no anaesthetics to fight the pain and no antibiotics to stop infection. The patient was likely to die from shock or infection.

13 Death

Tudor **courtiers** and **nobles** liked to mark their deaths in some special way. To be remembered, many left money to set up schools or **almshouses** for the poor to live in. Others left money to the poor or to the **Church**. Their families set up grand tombs to remember them by.

The widow of one courtier, Sir Henry Unton, remembered him in a painting which she had made. The painting on this page shows some of the important things that happened in Unton's life. It tells the story of the life of one of the many minor courtiers under Queen Elizabeth I. Use the diagram to follow the story of his life on the painting.

Source A

1 Unton as a baby with his mother. He was born in about 1557. The lady on the right is his nurse, who would have looked after him most of the time.

2 Unton went to Oxford University in 1573. Like many other young nobles and **gentlemen** he did not take a degree but moved on to the **Inns of Court**, (not shown in the picture) the London colleges for studying law.

3 Unton went on a tour of Europe. Italy and the Alps are shown on the picture. He came back to England in about 1578.

4 Unton is shown in each of the rooms in his house. You can see him in his study at the top of the house, feasting and watching a musical entertainment, playing music and talking about books with his friends. He spent as much time at home as he could, but was often needed at **Court**, where he worked for Sir Christopher Hatton. He was also an **MP** and a **Justice of the Peace**.

5 In 1585 Unton went to fight the Spanish in the Netherlands. He is shown wearing armour.

6 In 1591 Elizabeth I sent Unton to France as an **ambassador**. He fell ill and came home.

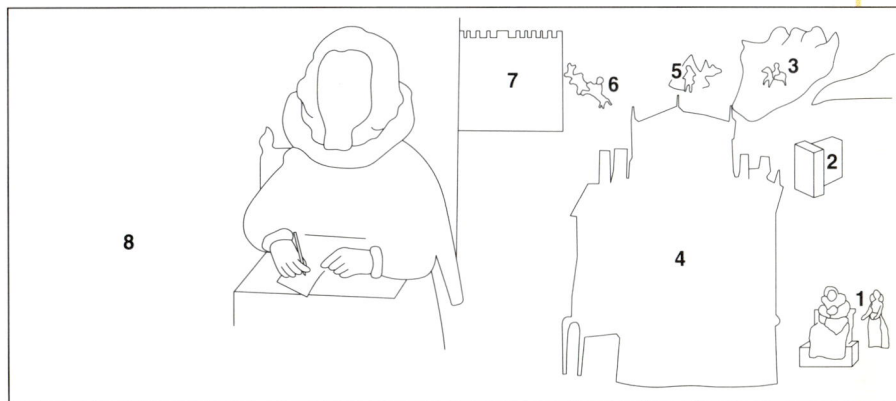

7 Unton did not go back to France. He took up his old life. In 1593 he spoke in Parliament against a royal tax. The Queen was furious, and banned him from Court. In 1595 she said she would forgive him and give him an important Court **place**, if he went to France again. He caught a **fever** there and died.

8 Unton's funeral takes up this part of the picture, with people mourning him. His grand tomb is also shown. The people sitting under the trees to the left of Unton's house are villagers mourning his death.

Glossary

almshouse a house built for the poor to live in, usually without paying any rent

ambassador A person sent by one monarch to another monarch to sort out a problem. Sometimes ambassadors went to live in a foreign country and went to Court there regularly.

appoint give a job to

archery shooting a bow and arrow

astrologer a person who gives advice about people's lives, based on the movements of the planets

border where two countries meet

cardinal A very important priest in the Roman Catholic Church. The cardinals choose the next Pope when one Pope dies.

chaplain a priest who holds private services for one family in their own chapel, not a public church

Church *either*: everyone belonging to a particular religion
   or: the system set up to run a particular religion

clerk a person who works for someone else, dealing with their letters and papers

coral rocky outer skeleton of tiny sea creatures

corrupted made to act dishonestly or disloyally

Court the monarch and the people who live and work with him or her

courtier a person who lives and works with the monarch

divorce legally break up a marriage

duties things that you have to do for other people

estate houses and lands that all belong to one family

fever an illness where the sick person gets very hot

gentleman a man with an income of between £500 and £700 a year

grammar school A school for boys, paid for by local people, not the government. They taught Latin and possibly Greek.

hawking using a trained hawk to catch birds, like pigeons, and bring them back to its owner

household everyone living in a house – the family and their servants

horoscope a prediction of what will happen to a person, based on where the planets were when that person was born and when the horoscope is worked out

Inns of Court the law schools of London which trained lawyers and also taught law to people who wanted to work in the government

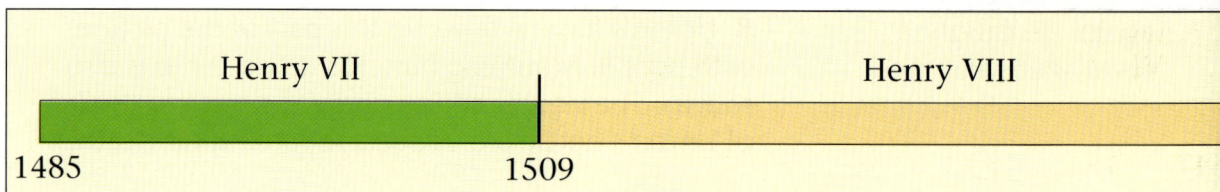

Henry VII	Henry VIII
1485	1509

invade to send an army into another country to try to take it over

joust to practice fighting on horseback

judgement in this quote the word means in the Queen's opinion

Justice of the Peace (JP) A person chosen by the monarch to make sure the law is being carried out in the part of the country where they live. JPs also ran the local law courts that dealt with unimportant crimes like fighting, running beer houses without a licence and stealing things that were not worth much.

MP someone chosen as a Member of Parliament

monarch a king or queen

noble One of the most important families in the country after the monarch. All nobles had a title, like 'Lord' or 'the Duke of'.

patron A person who helps someone else. Patrons were more important than the person they were helping. They might help by asking for favours or a job from someone even more important.

place a job at Court

plate plates, cups, bowls, jugs etc. made out of silver or gold

Pope The head of the Roman Catholic Church. All Roman Catholics, no matter what country they lived in, had to obey the Pope. If the Pope and the monarch of their country wanted different things, Roman Catholics were supposed to obey the Pope, not the monarch.

priest the person who holds the services in a church

Privy Council people, usually nobles, chosen by the monarch to give advice about running the country

promotion getting a more important job

quail small wild birds

rights things you can expect other people to do for you

sewage water and toilet contents

sewers tunnels to take away sewage

superior a person with either a more important job or a more important family

swaddle To wrap a baby in strips of cloth, like an Egyptian mummy. Swaddling kept babies still and quiet, and was said to help their bones grow straight.

tapestry a piece of cloth with a picture woven onto it

teething when teeth grow through a baby's gums

treason acting against the monarch of the country you live in

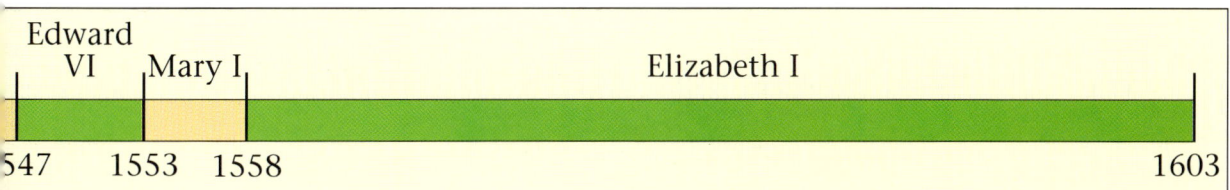

Edward VI	Mary I	Elizabeth I	
1547	1553	1558	1603

INDEX

Plain numbers (3) refer to the text. **Bold numbers (3)** refer to a source. Italic numbers (*3*) refer to a picture. Underlined numbers (<u>3</u>) refer to an information box.